I WANT TO BE A
NURSE

Written by
Jonathan Reule

Illustration
Novel Varius

Storyboard
Christiane Tee

UNIBINO
BOOKS

First paperback edition May 2023
ISBN 978-981-18-7136-8

Published by Unibino Pte. Ltd.
31 Rochester Drive Level 3, #03-47 Singapore 138637

www.unibino.com

Nurses are great caregivers in our society. These professionals are often on their feet, rushing around to help sick and injured patients who are in need of their care. It takes a strong individual to become a nurse, but it's a profession our world has needed for ages and will continue to need long into the future.

Perhaps you're considering a career in nursing? If that's the case, there are a few important things to know about this field. Being a nurse can often be a tough job. You'll need to have a strong mind, a determined spirit, and the ability to care for sick and sometimes dying patients.

But did you know that nursing is one of the oldest practices around? That's not to say that ancient nurses used to work in big hospitals as they do in our modern world, but the formation of the profession started thousands of years ago when there were young infants in need, and their mothers were unable to feed them.

The first nurses were what we now call 'wet nurses.' These women help offer breastmilk to other people's babies when the mothers have either passed away in childbirth or cannot produce enough milk to feed their children. These wet nurses were kind mothers who would take helpless infants into their care, at least long enough until the children could eat solid foods.

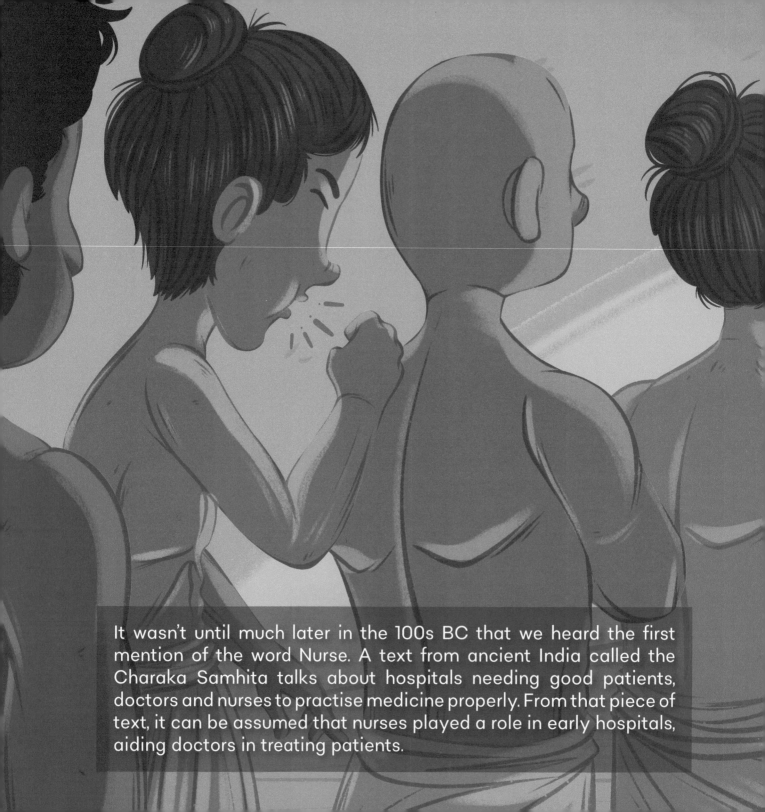

It wasn't until much later in the 100s BC that we heard the first mention of the word Nurse. A text from ancient India called the Charaka Samhita talks about hospitals needing good patients, doctors and nurses to practise medicine properly. From that piece of text, it can be assumed that nurses played a role in early hospitals, aiding doctors in treating patients.

The text continues to say that the nurse must be the following: knowledgeable when making medications for patients, clean in their practice, and kindhearted to all in the hospital's care. This sounds similar to modern-day nurses who often need to prepare medications to administer to patients. They also needed to be knowledgeable in the medical field before handling medicinal brews made at those times!

However, in the middle ages, nursing became a little more widespread as a profession. At those times, there were churches, synagogues, mosques, and temples that offered basic care for the sick and elderly. But these establishments rarely had any medical treatments, only nuns and nurses to watch over the patients.

For many centuries these establishments took the place of public health systems, even if the nurses there could only offer sympathy to the sick and elderly. This tradition slowly began dying down as religious institutions' beliefs changed over time. Many of these establishments started to close their doors to patients, leaving a gap in nursing history for many years to come.

That is until the 1800s, during the Crimean War when Florence Nightingale gave nursing a big boost from its low period. As she went onto the battlefields to tend to wounded soldiers, she found that the nursing conditions were dreadfully lacking, but she didn't let this deter her from doing the best she could manage. Because of her determination, she eventually came to be known as the 'lady with the lamp' during the war.

Although, it was after the war that Florence grew inspired to write a three-volume book titled Notes on Nursing. This helped to lay a structured foundation for the practice of nursing. But her biggest feat came a year later when Queen Elizabeth requested the construction of an Army Nurse's hospital, where Florence was asked to oversee the training of the nurses and its overall operations.

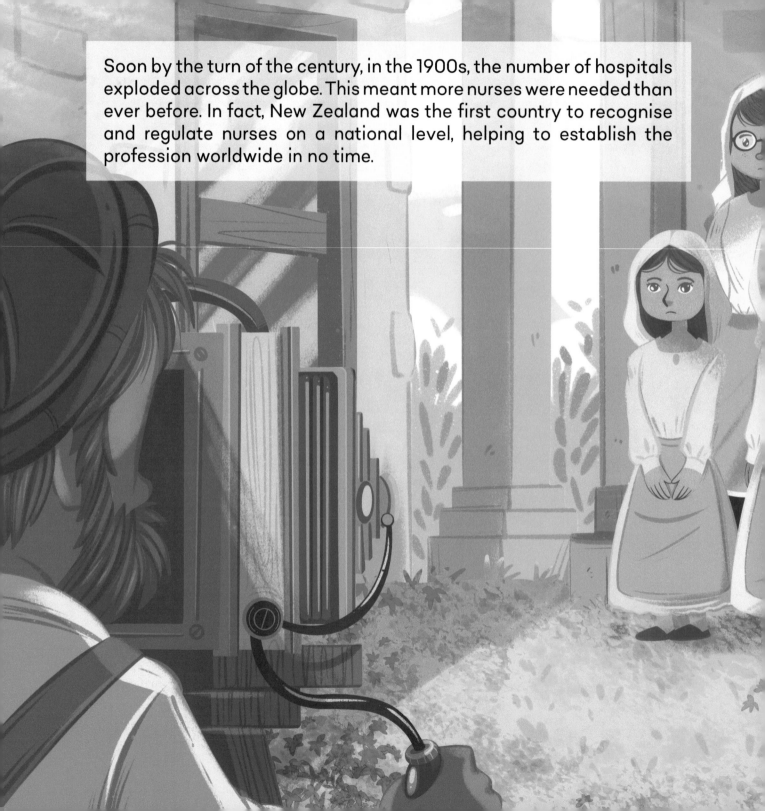

Soon by the turn of the century, in the 1900s, the number of hospitals exploded across the globe. This meant more nurses were needed than ever before. In fact, New Zealand was the first country to recognise and regulate nurses on a national level, helping to establish the profession worldwide in no time.

As the field of medicine grew and bloomed, it opened up more and more jobs for nurses, which also brought about better nursing schools, training programs, and working conditions. Nurses started to take a more prominent role in hospitals by becoming the emissary between doctors and patients.

But what do nurses do in our modern world? What are their roles in hospitals and other medical practices? For nurses nowadays, this can be a wide variety of tasks and responsibilities.

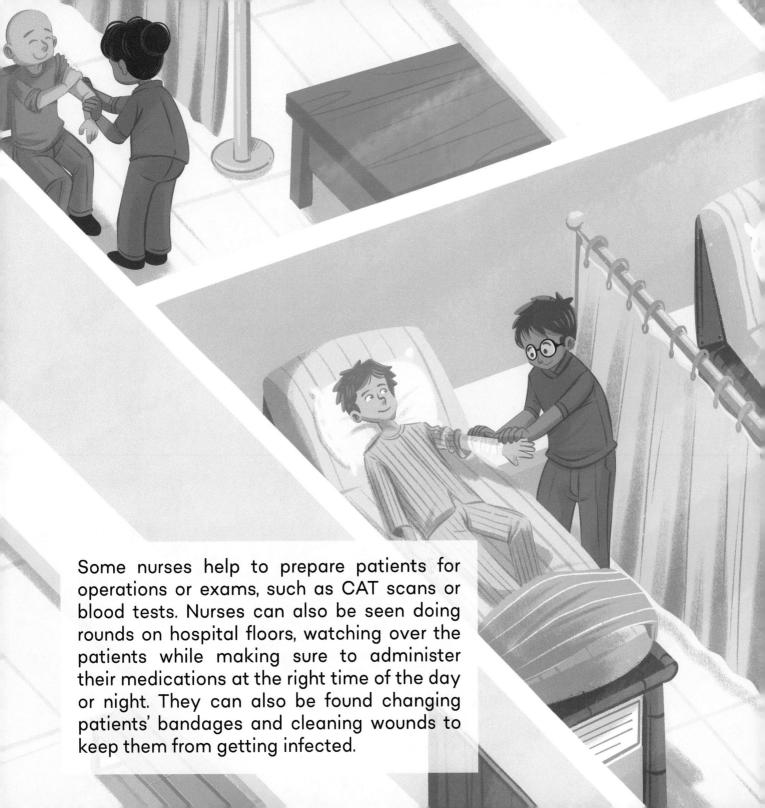

Some nurses help to prepare patients for operations or exams, such as CAT scans or blood tests. Nurses can also be seen doing rounds on hospital floors, watching over the patients while making sure to administer their medications at the right time of the day or night. They can also be found changing patients' bandages and cleaning wounds to keep them from getting infected.

Being a nurse isn't always the easiest job. It requires time studying, dedication to the profession, and a strong will when faced with daily challenges that arise for nurses. But that's why we need nurses in our hospitals and other healthcare establishments.

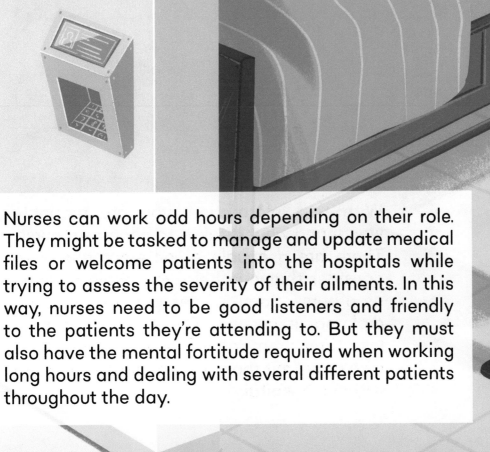

Nurses can work odd hours depending on their role. They might be tasked to manage and update medical files or welcome patients into the hospitals while trying to assess the severity of their ailments. In this way, nurses need to be good listeners and friendly to the patients they're attending to. But they must also have the mental fortitude required when working long hours and dealing with several different patients throughout the day.

With this information, you are probably wondering what it takes to become a nurse. There are a couple of different routes to consider that can help you begin working as a nurse. Some nurses get a specialised diploma in nursing. These diplomas take less time than earning a degree, but they also may limit the roles a nurse can perform within a hospital.

Nowadays, most hospitals prefer their nurses to have at least a bachelor's degree in Nursing. In some cases, hospitals may even require nurses to obtain a master's degree before being hired. So if you want to be a nurse, it's important to study hard and learn as much as possible in your classes.

After that, there are a few other practical matters to consider before taking a job as a registered nurse. Know that nursing often requires a certain level of physical stamina. Most nurses have to be on their feet during their shifts, walking between beds and checking on the various patients within the hospital, which can amount to a lot of walking by the end of their days.

Nursing also requires emotional fortitude. Not all patients will be easy to deal with. Some may be suffering from diseases that cause them to be forgetful or even act in an antisocial manner. Aspiring nurses must also come to grips with the reality that some patients will pass away no matter how well they've taken care of them throughout their stay.

But why don't we have a look at the different types of nurses to have a better picture of the profession as a whole? Orthopaedic nurses work with the musco-skeletal system. This could be in surgery or other non-surgical treatments. Imagine a person who has broken their arm or a sports player with a torn ligament.

An ears, eyes, nose, and throat nurse usually works with the general public when any of these areas above are affected by injuries or diseases. You'll normally find an ENT nurse working in a clinic alongside a family doctor, who can see a host of patients on any given day. ENT nurses often find themselves dealing with more minor illnesses, such as colds, runny noses, and ear and eye infections.

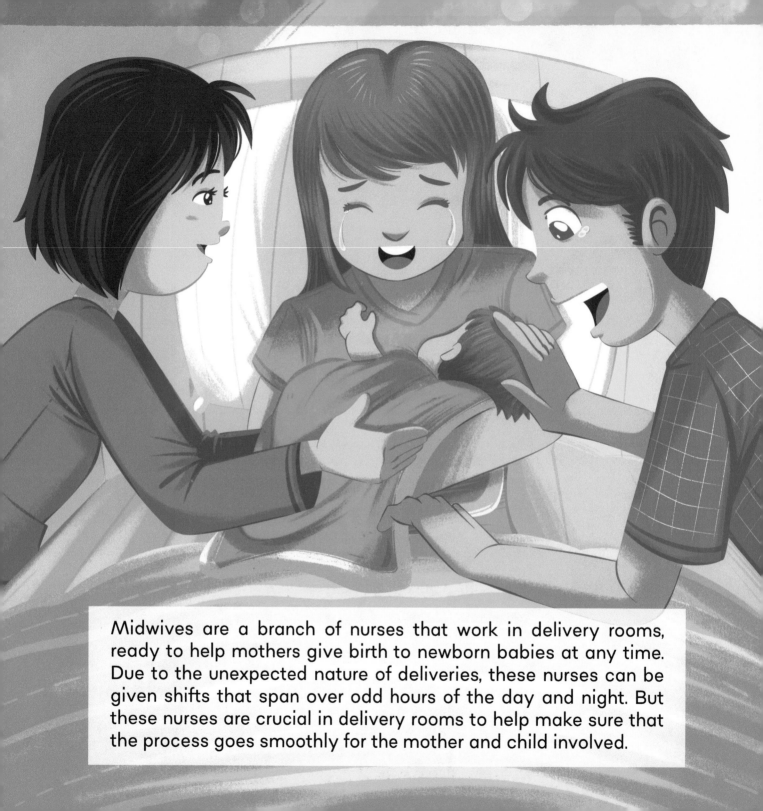

Midwives are a branch of nurses that work in delivery rooms, ready to help mothers give birth to newborn babies at any time. Due to the unexpected nature of deliveries, these nurses can be given shifts that span over odd hours of the day and night. But these nurses are crucial in delivery rooms to help make sure that the process goes smoothly for the mother and child involved.

Paediatric nurses work primarily with children. Since children are shaped differently than adults, they will need specialised treatments to match their developing bodies.

Emergency room nurses are living life in the fast lane. These nurses rarely know what type of patient might be brought into their care. Emergency room nurses need to have a wide range of knowledge about various infections, diseases, and injuries in order to make quick decisions. Nurses who work in this environment should be someone who can think on their toes, no matter what problems may arise in their day.

Oncological nurses work closely with cancer patients, helping to give them their medication when scheduled, encouraging them, and ensuring the patient rooms stay sterile and free from unwanted germs. Oncological nurses can end up spending a long amount of time with the patients in their care, depending on the length of treatment for each patient. These nurses should be strong emotionally and mentally, as this field can at times have success stories and at others unfortunate passings.

Nurses are also essential for keeping things moving at mental health facilities. On an average day, they might help administer medications to patients or keep patients with memory loss on a fixed schedule, especially if they've forgotten what time it is. These nurses also help keep records organised and tidy for all the patients while overseeing operations in these facilities.

Another vital role is that of a nurse manager. These professionals are in charge of the many business aspects involved with nursing. They can be found creating schedules for the nurses in their wards or focusing on how to make their work more efficient. They usually are found between the nurses and hospital executives to ensure everyone is on the same page about daily operations.

Being a nurse can be a challenging yet rewarding career. As our world keeps expanding, so will our hospitals and clinics, requiring passionate nurses who are dedicated to helping patients from all walks of life. If you feel that you've got the right mind and personality, then perhaps you can consider a career in nursing.

As you can see, nursing is one of the oldest professions around and will continue to be important long into the future. Remember to study hard and progress toward your goal one step at a time. But if you are keen to work in the medical field as a registered nurse, nothing can stop you from achieving your dreams!

My Inspiration

Shubhi Saxena
Founder, Unibino

As a parent in this ever-changing world, it can sometimes feel overwhelming when it comes to our children's futures. New technologies seem to be arising almost every day, and with so many innovations, it creates unique professions which many of us wouldn't have dreamed to be necessary only a few years ago. Which to me is a good thing. Because with so much variety, my children can have the opportunity to pick a career that will fit their personalities and build upon their strengths. As you may imagine, this desire within me to provide my children with the resources they needed to thrive, led me to search out books that would be easy enough for them to understand while teaching them about various professions.

Only, I found that these books were few and far between. Even if I could find a book about a certain profession geared towards young readers, I found them sparse inside and limited to only certain careers that may not fit my children's abilities. This is when I came up with the idea to write my own children's books, teaching them about all the various careers in the modern world. After months of researching different professions and learning more than I ever expected, I quickly realised this was going to be a bigger project than I first anticipated. I dove into the histories of these professions, discovering links to the past, and why these professions were now so important.

Ultimately my goal was to offer my children options, to show them that there is no one set path for everyone. But in this, I stumbled upon something bigger. I wanted to share this with future generations. To share with all children and parents about these careers, to help spark curiosity, and to instil a passion for the future. Everyone has special talents and abilities, and I hope that this series will be able to offer clarity and inspiration to children around the world. Because at the end of the day, it's never too early to start dreaming and never too late to take action. With this, I hope you enjoy this series and that your young ones become the best versions of themselves as they can achieve.

Printed in the USA
CPSIA information can be obtained
at www.ICGtesting.com
LVHW060244231123
764447LV00025B/92